MY WEEKLY MASS JOURNAL

52 WEEKS OF CREATIVE NOTE-TAKING FOR CATHOLIC BOYS AGES 7 +

TO PARENTS & GUARDIAN

"Train up a child in the way he should go, And when he is old he will not depart from it."

Proverbs 22:6

TO CHILDREN

"Children, obey your parents in the Lord, for this is right. "Honor your father and mother," which is the first commandment with a promise: "that it may be well with you, and you may live long on the earth."

Ephesians 6:1-4

MY WEEKLY MASS JOURNAL

52 Weeks of Creative Note — Taking
for Catholic Boys Ages 7+

ISBN: 9798743171033

This Weekly Mass Journal belongs to:

_____

_____

Help your kids focus on Sunday Masses in the most creative and engaging way!

This Catholic Mass Journal provides **104 uniquely designed pages** with faith-based and interactive questions before, during, and after the Mass. This will help you keep your kid's mind active while focusing on Sunday Masses.

This Catholic Mass Journal also acts as a keepsake to record your kid's notes and thoughts that they can look back on for years to come.

Key Features of our Book

Holds 52 Weeks of Mass Sheets
(2 Beautiful Pages for Each Mass)

Page 1   NON-REPETITIVE DESIGNS   Page 2

Our design provides different themes and activities that your kids might enjoy doing whether it is sports-related, self-care, love for animals, love for nature, and any other interesting activities.

At the end of the mass, your kids will learn to listen, reflect, learn and apply the word of God in their lives.

We are happy to help! We appreciate a review and feedback from you! Be blessed and be a blessing!

It's good to know things!

WHAT CAN I PRAY ABOUT?

Anything! Nothing is too big or too small.

WHAT DOES THE SIGN OF THE CROSS MEAN?

It is a way we call upon God in everything that we do. We are remembering that there are three (3) Persons in 1 (one) God also known as the Holy Trinity.

VESTMENTS COLORS & MEANING

- **Green** – Ordinary time, symbolizes the hope & life of each new day
- **Purple** – Advent & Lent, represents penance, preparation, & sacrifice

- **Rose/Pink** – Middle of both Advent & Lent, worn on these days to show the joy & love in God
- **White/Gold** – Easter and Christmas, symbolized the birth and resurrection

- **Red** – Pentecost Sunday and Palm Sunday, symbolizes the passion & blood of Christ
- **Blue** – Marian feast day, worn only once a year
- **Black** – All Souls, Funeral Masses

SHOULD I PRAY A LOUD?

God hears you whether you pray aloud or silently.

HOW DO YOU SAY THE SIGN OF THE CROSS?

Hands together.
"In the name of the Father, and of the Son, and of the Holy Spirit. Amen"

Right hand on your forehead for the word "FATHER"

On your left shoulder for the word "HOLY"

On your right shoulder for the word "SPIRIT"

1
3   4
2

In the middle of your chest for the word "SON"

My Mass Journal

Today's Date:

Liturgical Calendar:

Responsorial Psalm:

Today I heard the Gospel according to:

How do you attend/watch the mass?

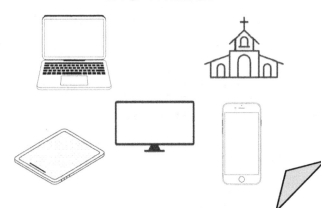

I'm with my:

Words I don't know:

THE PRIEST'S MESSAGE:

3 BIG THINGS I LEARNED TODAY:

DRAW A PICTURE OR WRITE SOMETHING YOU HEARD FROM THE GOSPEL

MASS JOURNAL

Date: _____

Priest: _____

1st Reading: _____

2nd Reading: _____

WHERE IS THE GOSPEL READING FROM?

_____

3 NAMES OR CHARACTERS I HEARD:

1.

2.

3.

WHAT ARE YOU LEARNING ABOUT GOD FROM THE HOMILY?

I can apply this in my life by..

MY FAVORITE WORSHIP SONG TODAY:

FUTURE PILOT!

TODAY WE PRAY FOR:

SOMETHING I LEARNED ABOUT MYSELF

My Sunday Notes

Today's
Date:

Gospel according to:

Priest:

What color are the priest's vestments today?

WHAT I LEARNED

The gospel story was about:

What does God want me to learn?

How should I change because of this homily?

My favorite church song today:

Today I want to pray for:

DRAW A PICTURE OR WRITE SOMETHING YOU HEARD IN THE GOSPEL

GO TEAM

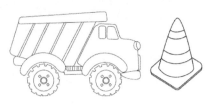 

My Sunday Mass Notes

	YES!	NO!
Did you read your Bible this week?	☐	☐
Did you still remember last week's sermon?	☐	☐
Can you say a verse you have learned recently?	☐	☐

Gospel according to: Today's date:

CATCH THE WORD: Check the box each time you hear the word.

☐ God   ☐ Israel   ☐ House
☐ Love   ☐ People   ☐ Day
☐ Jesus   ☐ King   ☐ People
☐ Man   ☐ Son   ☐ Disciples

TODAY'S GOSPEL IS ABOUT..

APPLICATION

I should..

I should not..

DRAW A PICTURE OF SOMETHING YOU HEARD IN THE GOSPEL

My Mass Journal

Today's Date:

Liturgical Calendar:

Responsorial Psalm:

Today I heard the Gospel according to:

How do you attend/watch the mass?

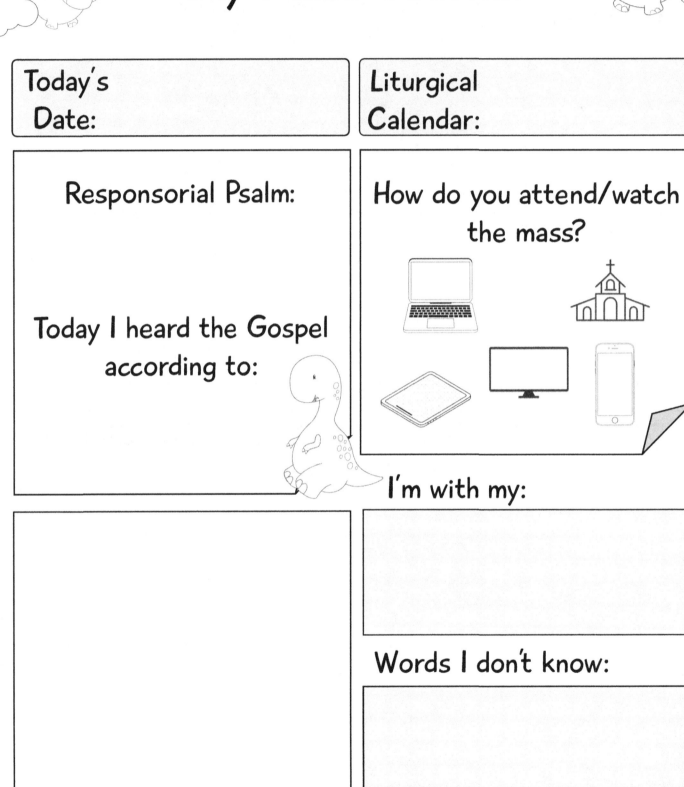

I'm with my:

Words I don't know:

THE PRIEST'S MESSAGE:

3 BIG THINGS I LEARNED TODAY:

DRAW A PICTURE OR WRITE SOMETHING YOU HEARD FROM THE GOSPEL

MASS JOURNAL SHEET

Date:_____ Priest:_____

1st Reading: _____ 2nd Reading: _____

WHERE IS THE GOSPEL READING FROM?

_____

3 NAMES OR CHARACTERS I HEARD:

1.

2.

3.

WHAT ARE YOU LEARNING ABOUT GOD FROM THE HOMILY?

I can apply this in my life by..

MY FAVORITE WORSHIP SONG TODAY:

Happy Robots!

TODAY WE PRAY FOR:

SOMETHING I LEARNED ABOUT MYSELF

My Sunday Notes

Today's
Date:

Gospel according to:

Priest:

What color are the priest's
vestments today?

WHAT I LEARNED

The gospel story was about:

What does God want me to
learn?

How should I change because of
this homily?

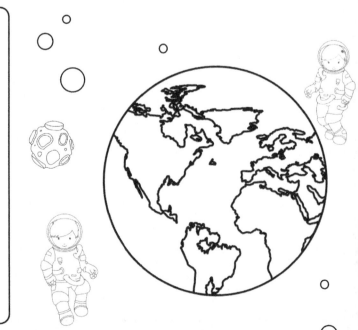

My favorite church song today:

Today I want to pray for:

DRAW A PICTURE OR WRITE SOMETHING
YOU HEARD IN THE GOSPEL

My Sunday Mass Notes

	YES!	NO!
Did you read your Bible this week?	☐	☐
Did you still remember last week's sermon?	☐	☐
Can you say a verse you have learned recently?	☐	☐

Gospel according to: Today's date:

CATCH THE WORD: Check the box each time you hear the word.

☐ God   ☐ Israel   ☐ House
☐ Love   ☐ People   ☐ Day
☐ Jesus   ☐ King   ☐ People
☐ Man   ☐ Son   ☐ Disciples

TODAY'S GOSPEL IS ABOUT..

APPLICATION

I should..

I should not..

DRAW A PICTURE OF SOMETHING YOU HEARD IN THE GOSPEL

My Mass Journal

Today's Date:

Liturgical Calendar:

Responsorial Psalm:

Today I heard the Gospel according to:

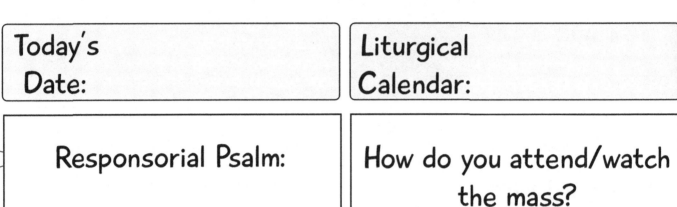

How do you attend/watch the mass?

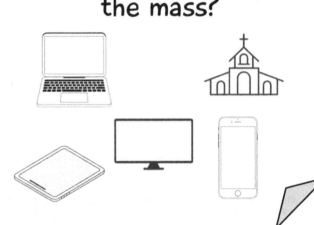

I'm with my:

Words I don't know:

THE PRIEST'S MESSAGE:

3 BIG THINGS I LEARNED TODAY:

DRAW A PICTURE OR WRITE SOMETHING YOU HEARD FROM THE GOSPEL

MASS JOURNAL SHEET

Date: _____   Priest: _____

1st Reading: _____   2nd Reading: _____

WHERE IS THE GOSPEL
READING FROM?

_____

3 NAMES OR CHARACTERS I HEARD:

1.

2.

3.

WHAT ARE YOU LEARNING ABOUT GOD FROM THE HOMILY?

I can apply this in my life by..

MY FAVORITE WORSHIP SONG TODAY:

TODAY WE PRAY FOR:

SOMETHING I LEARNED ABOUT MYSELF

My Sunday Notes

Today's
Date:

Gospel according to:

Priest:

What color are the priest's
vestments today?

WHAT I LEARNED

The gospel story was about:

What does God want me to
learn?

How should I change because of
this homily?

My favorite church song today:

Today I want to pray for:

DRAW A PICTURE OR WRITE SOMETHING
YOU HEARD IN THE GOSPEL

My Sunday Mass Notes

	YES!	NO!
Did you read your Bible this week?	☐	☐
Did you still remember last weeks sermon?	☐	☐
Can you say a verse you have learned recently?	☐	☐

Gospel according to: Today's date:

CATCH THE WORD: Check the box each time you hear the word.

☐ God   ☐ Israel   ☐ House
☐ Love   ☐ People   ☐ Day
☐ Jesus   ☐ King   ☐ People
☐ Man   ☐ Son   ☐ Disciples

TODAY'S GOSPEL IS ABOUT..

APPLICATION

I should..

I should not..

DRAW A PICTURE OF SOMETHING YOU HEARD IN THE GOSPEL

My Mass Journal

Today's Date:

Liturgical Calendar:

Responsorial Psalm:

Today I heard the Gospel according to:

How do you attend/watch the mass?

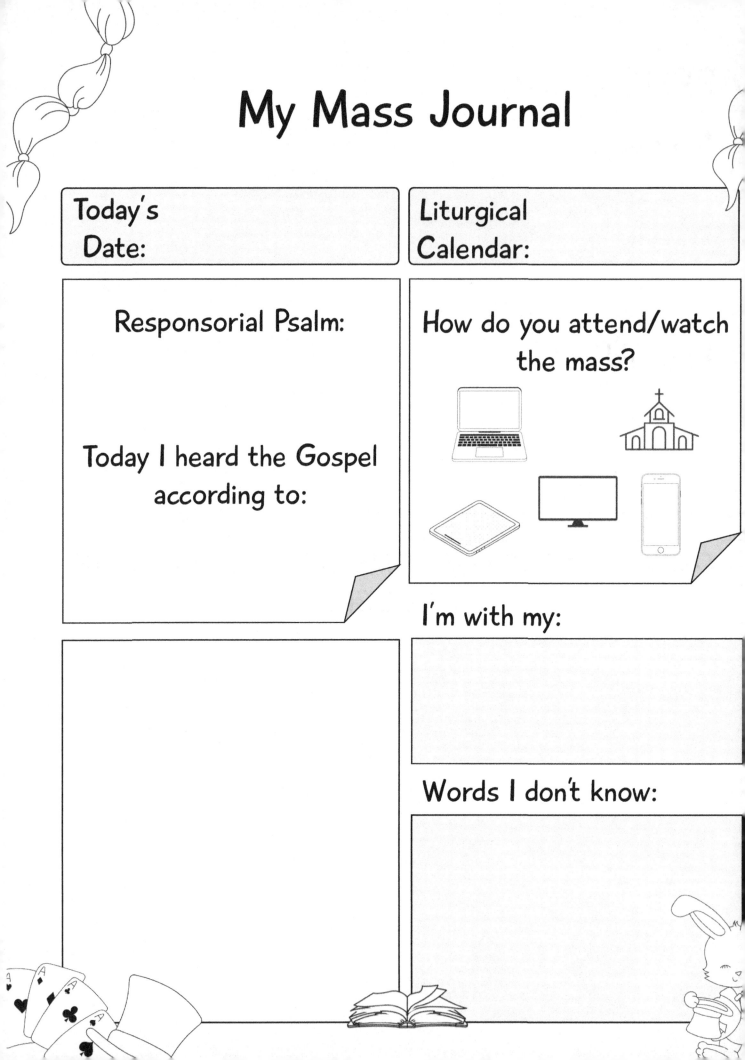

I'm with my:

Words I don't know:

THE PRIEST'S MESSAGE:

3 BIG THINGS I LEARNED TODAY:

DRAW A PICTURE OR WRITE SOMETHING YOU HEARD FROM THE GOSPEL

MASS JOURNAL SHEET

Date: _____   Priest: _____

1st Reading: _____   2nd Reading: _____

WHERE IS THE GOSPEL READING FROM?

_____

3 NAMES OR CHARACTERS I HEARD:

1.

2.

3.

WHAT ARE YOU LEARNING ABOUT GOD FROM THE HOMILY?

I can apply this in my life by..

MY FAVORITE
WORSHIP SONG TODAY:

TODAY WE
PRAY FOR:

SOMETHING I LEARNED ABOUT MYSELF

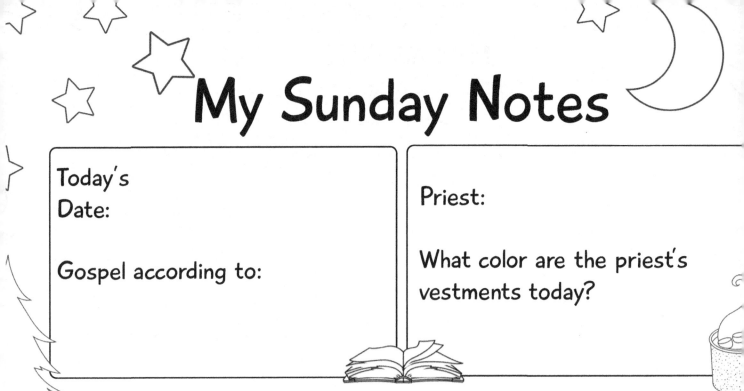

My Sunday Notes

Today's
Date:

Gospel according to:

Priest:

What color are the priest's vestments today?

WHAT I LEARNED

The gospel story was about:

What does God want me to learn?

How should I change because of this homily?

CAMP LIFE!

My favorite church song today:

Today I want to pray for:

DRAW A PICTURE OR WRITE SOMETHING
YOU HEARD IN THE GOSPEL

My Sunday Mass Notes

	YES!	NO!
Did you read your Bible this week?	☐	☐
Did you still remember last week's sermon?	☐	☐
Can you say a verse you have learned recently?	☐	☐

Gospel according to: Today's date:

CATCH THE WORD: Check the box each time you hear the word.

☐ God	☐ Israel	☐ House
☐ Love	☐ People	☐ Day
☐ Jesus	☐ King	☐ People
☐ Man	☐ Son	☐ Disciples

TODAY'S GOSPEL IS ABOUT..

APPLICATION

I should..

I should not..

DRAW A PICTURE OF SOMETHING YOU HEARD IN THE GOSPEL

My Mass Journal

Today's Date:

Liturgical Calendar:

Responsorial Psalm:

Today I heard the Gospel according to:

How do you attend/watch the mass?

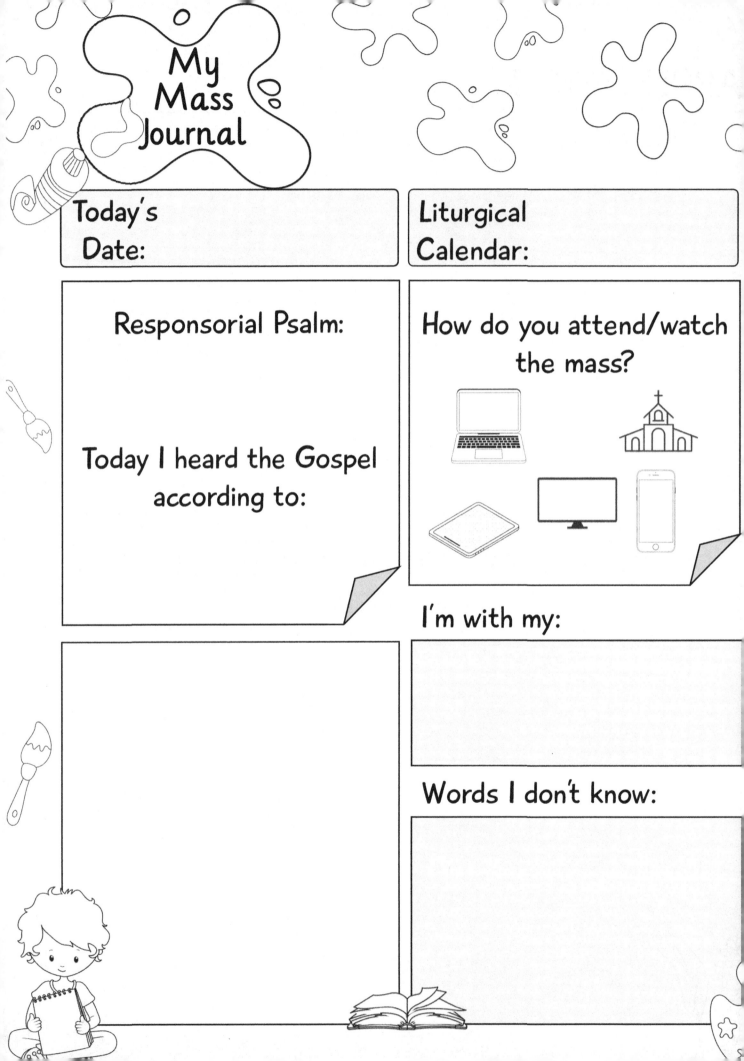

I'm with my:

Words I don't know:

THE PRIEST'S MESSAGE:

3 BIG THINGS I LEARNED TODAY:

DRAW A PICTURE OR WRITE SOMETHING YOU HEARD FROM THE GOSPEL

MASS JOURNAL SHEET

Date:_____   Priest:_____

1st Reading: _____   2nd Reading: _____

WHERE IS THE GOSPEL READING FROM?

_____

3 NAMES OR CHARACTERS I HEARD:

1.

2.

3.

WHAT ARE YOU LEARNING ABOUT GOD FROM THE HOMILY?

I can apply this in my life by..

APPLE PICKING!

MY FAVORITE WORSHIP SONG TODAY:

TODAY WE PRAY FOR:

SOMETHING I LEARNED ABOUT MYSELF

My Sunday Notes

Today's
Date:

Gospel according to:

Priest:

What color are the priest's vestments today?

WHAT I LEARNED

The gospel story was about:

What does God want me to learn?

How should I change because of this homily?

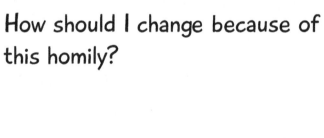

POPCORN

CIRCUS LIFE!

My favorite church song today:

Today I want to pray for:

DRAW A PICTURE OR WRITE SOMETHING
YOU HEARD IN THE GOSPEL

My Sunday Mass Notes

	YES!	NO!
Did you read your Bible this week?	☐	☐
Did you still remember last week's sermon?	☐	☐
Can you say a verse you have learned recently?	☐	☐

Gospel according to: _____   Today's date: _____

CATCH THE WORD: Check the box each time you hear the word.

☐ God   ☐ Israel   ☐ House
☐ Love   ☐ People   ☐ Day
☐ Jesus   ☐ King   ☐ People
☐ Man   ☐ Son   ☐ Disciples

TODAY'S GOSPEL IS ABOUT..

APPLICATION

I should..

I should not..

DRAW A PICTURE OF SOMETHING YOU HEARD IN THE GOSPEL

My Mass Journal

Today's Date:

Liturgical Calendar:

Responsorial Psalm:

Today I heard the Gospel according to:

How do you attend/watch the mass?

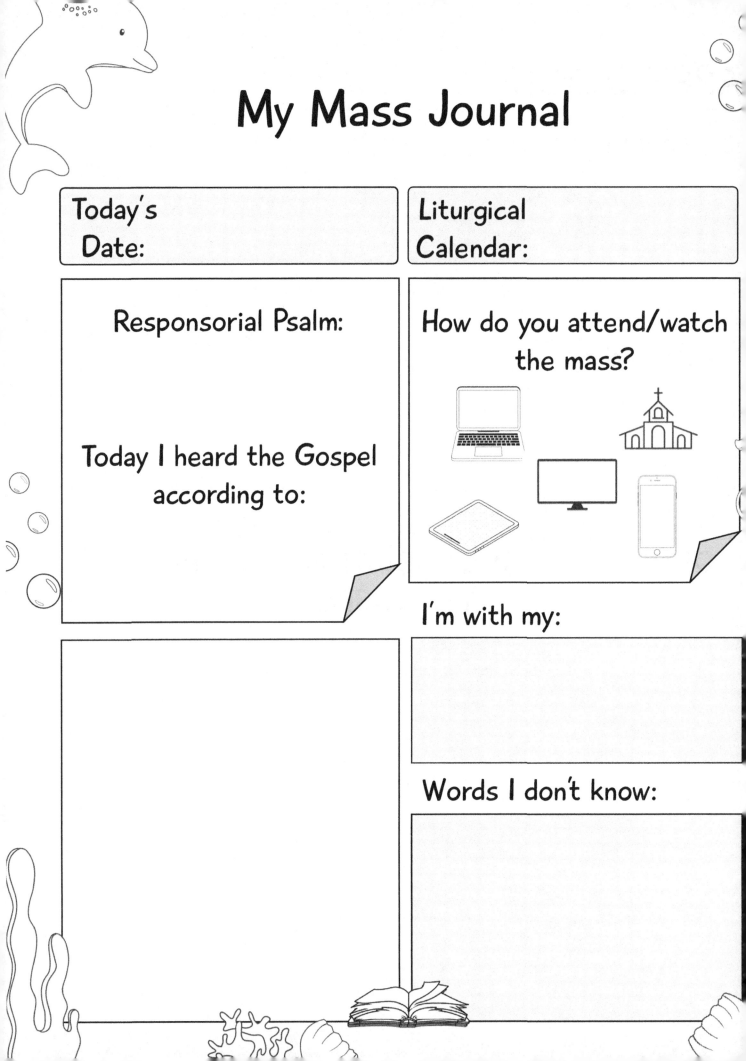

I'm with my:

Words I don't know:

THE PRIEST'S MESSAGE:

3 BIG THINGS I LEARNED TODAY:

DRAW A PICTURE OR WRITE SOMETHING YOU HEARD FROM THE GOSPEL

MASS JOURNAL SHEET

Date:_____   Priest:_____

1st Reading: _____   2nd Reading: _____

WHERE IS THE GOSPEL READING FROM?

_____

3 NAMES OR CHARACTERS I HEARD:

1.

2.

3.

WHAT ARE YOU LEARNING ABOUT GOD FROM THE HOMILY?

I can apply this in my life by..

MY FAVORITE WORSHIP SONG TODAY:

TODAY WE PRAY FOR:

SOMETHING I LEARNED ABOUT MYSELF

My Sunday Notes

Today's
Date:

Gospel according to:

Priest:

What color are the priest's vestments today?

WHAT I LEARNED

The gospel story was about:

What does God want me to learn?

How should I change because of this homily?

KARATE

My favorite church song today:

Today I want to pray for:

TRAIN

DRAW A PICTURE OR WRITE SOMETHING YOU HEARD IN THE GOSPEL

PROGRESS

My Sunday Mass Notes

	YES!	NO!
Did you read your Bible this week?	☐	☐
Did you still remember last week's sermon?	☐	☐
Can you say a verse you have learned recently?	☐	☐

Gospel according to: Today's date:

CATCH THE WORD: Check the box each time you hear the word.

☐ God   ☐ Israel   ☐ House
☐ Love   ☐ People   ☐ Day
☐ Jesus   ☐ King   ☐ People
☐ Man   ☐ Son   ☐ Disciples

TODAY'S GOSPEL IS ABOUT..

APPLICATION

I should..

I should not..

DRAW A PICTURE OF SOMETHING YOU HEARD IN THE GOSPEL

My Mass Journal

Today's Date:

Liturgical Calendar:

Responsorial Psalm:

Today I heard the Gospel according to:

How do you attend/watch the mass?

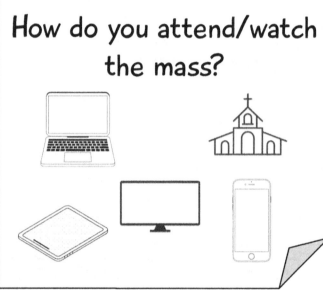

I'm with my:

Words I don't know:

THE PRIEST'S MESSAGE:

3 BIG THINGS I LEARNED TODAY:

DRAW A PICTURE OR WRITE SOMETHING YOU HEARD FROM THE GOSPEL

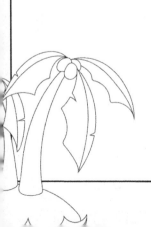

MASS JOURNAL SHEET

Date:_____   Priest:_____

1st Reading: _____   2nd Reading: _____

WHERE IS THE GOSPEL READING FROM?

_____

3 NAMES OR CHARACTERS I HEARD:

1.

2.

3.

WHAT ARE YOU LEARNING ABOUT GOD FROM THE HOMILY?

I can apply this in my life by..

POLICE

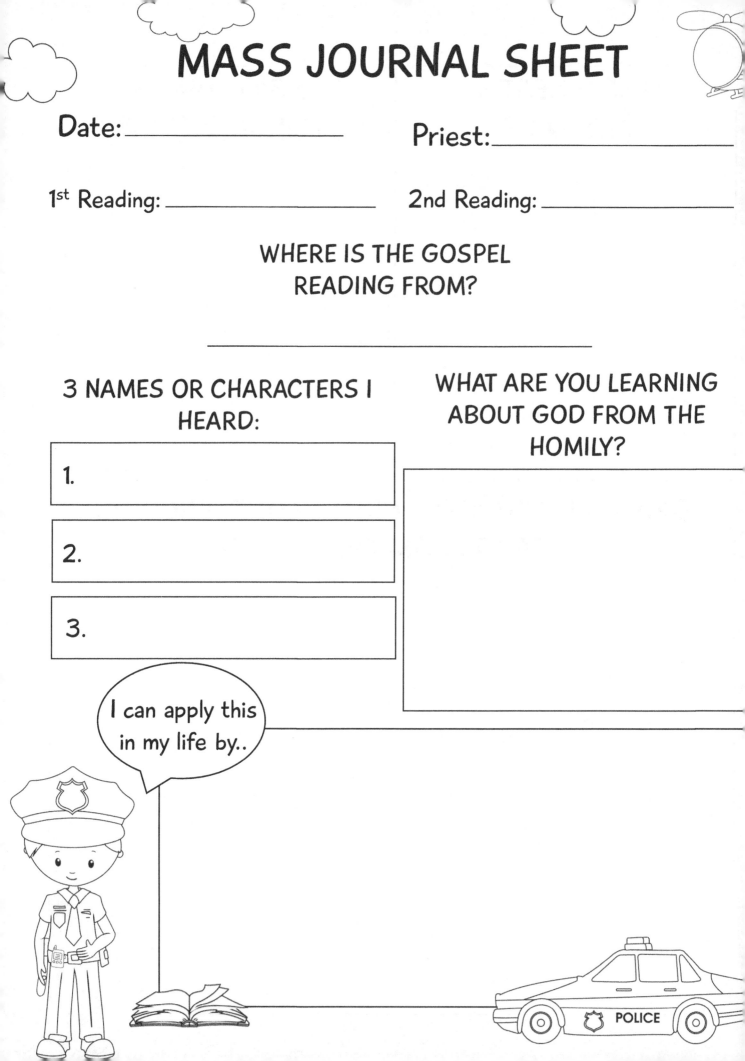

MY FAVORITE
WORSHIP SONG TODAY:

TODAY WE
PRAY FOR:

SOMETHING I LEARNED ABOUT MYSELF

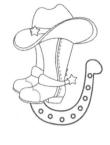

My Sunday Notes

Today's
Date:

Gospel according to:

Priest:

What color are the priest's vestments today?

WHAT I LEARNED

The gospel story was about:

What does God want me to learn?

How should I change because of this homily?

My favorite church song today:

Today I want to pray for:

DRAW A PICTURE OR WRITE SOMETHING
YOU HEARD IN THE GOSPEL

My Sunday Mass Notes

	YES!	NO!
Did you read your Bible this week?	☐	☐
Did you still remember last week's sermon?	☐	☐
Can you say a verse you have learned recently?	☐	☐

Gospel according to: Today's date:

CATCH THE WORD: Check the box each time you hear the word.

☐ God   ☐ Israel   ☐ House
☐ Love   ☐ People   ☐ Day
☐ Jesus   ☐ King   ☐ People
☐ Man   ☐ Son   ☐ Disciples

TODAY'S GOSPEL IS ABOUT..

APPLICATION

I should..

I should not..

DRAW A PICTURE OF SOMETHING YOU HEARD IN THE GOSPEL

My Mass Journal

Today's Date:

Liturgical Calendar:

Responsorial Psalm:

Today I heard the Gospel according to:

How do you attend/watch the mass?

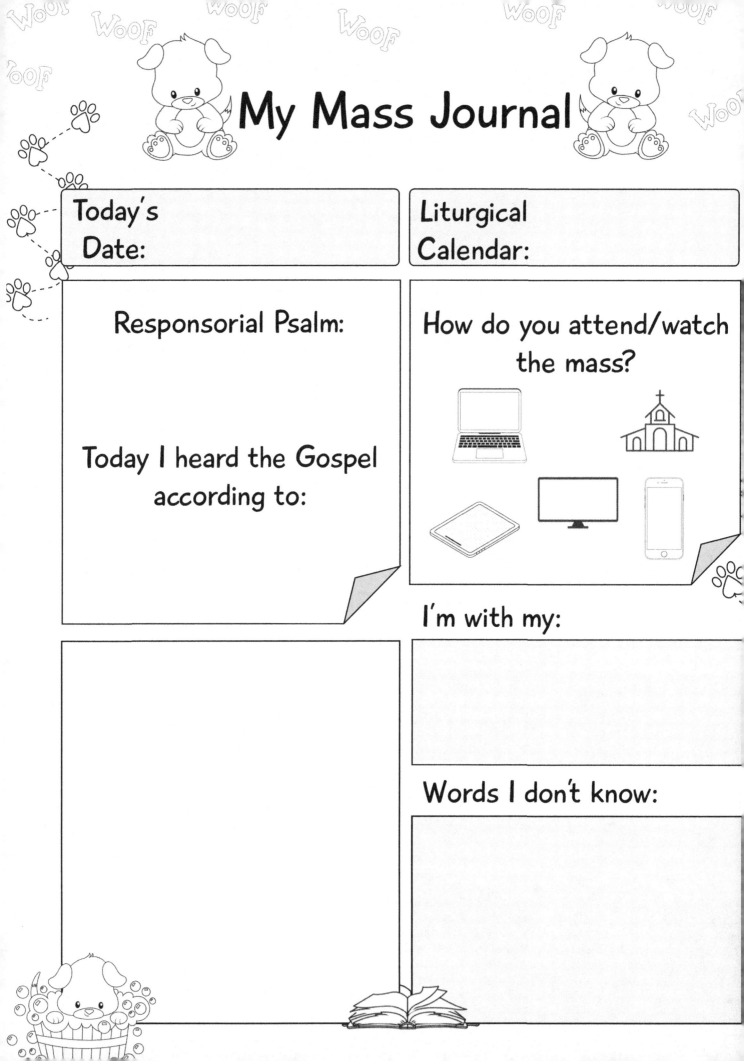

I'm with my:

Words I don't know:

THE PRIEST'S MESSAGE:

3 BIG THINGS I LEARNED TODAY:

DRAW A PICTURE OR WRITE SOMETHING YOU HEARD FROM THE GOSPEL

MASS JOURNAL SHEET

Date:_____ Priest:_____

1st Reading: _____ 2nd Reading: _____

WHERE IS THE GOSPEL READING FROM?

_____

3 NAMES OR CHARACTERS I HEARD:

1.

2.

3.

WHAT ARE YOU LEARNING ABOUT GOD FROM THE HOMILY?

PRAISE & WORSHIP

I can apply this in my life by..

MY FAVORITE WORSHIP SONG TODAY:

PRAISE & WORSHIP

TODAY WE PRAY FOR:

SOMETHING I LEARNED ABOUT MYSELF

My Sunday Notes

Today's
Date:

Gospel according to:

Priest:

What color are the priest's vestments today?

WHAT I LEARNED

The gospel story was about:

What does God want me to learn?

How should I change because of this homily?

My favorite church song today:

Today I want to pray for:

DRAW A PICTURE OR WRITE SOMETHING
YOU HEARD IN THE GOSPEL

My Sunday Mass Notes

	YES!	NO!
Did you read your Bible this week?	☐	☐
Did you still remember last week's sermon?	☐	☐
Can you say a verse you have learned recently?	☐	☐

Gospel according to: Today's date:

CATCH THE WORD: Check the box each time you hear the word.

☐ God	☐ Israel	☐ House
☐ Love	☐ People	☐ Day
☐ Jesus	☐ King	☐ People
☐ Man	☐ Son	☐ Disciples

TODAY'S GOSPEL IS ABOUT..

APPLICATION

I should..

I should not..

DRAW A PICTURE OF SOMETHING YOU HEARD IN THE GOSPEL

My Mass Journal

Today's Date:

Liturgical Calendar:

Responsorial Psalm:

Today I heard the Gospel according to:

How do you attend/watch the mass?

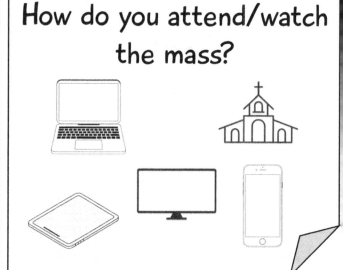

I'm with my:

Words I don't know:

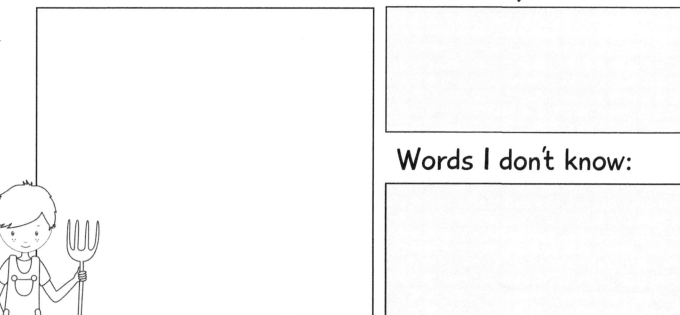

THE PRIEST'S MESSAGE:

3 BIG THINGS I LEARNED TODAY:

DRAW A PICTURE OR WRITE SOMETHING YOU HEARD FROM THE GOSPEL

BARN LIFE!

MASS JOURNAL SHEET

Date:_____   Priest:_____

1st Reading: _____   2nd Reading: _____

WHERE IS THE GOSPEL READING FROM?

_____

3 NAMES OR CHARACTERS I HEARD:

1.

2.

3.

WHAT ARE YOU LEARNING ABOUT GOD FROM THE HOMILY?

I can apply this in my life by..

MY FAVORITE WORSHIP SONG TODAY:

MOVIE NIGHT

ADMIT ONE
ADMIT ONE

TODAY WE PRAY FOR:

SOMETHING I LEARNED ABOUT MYSELF

My Sunday Notes

Today's
Date:

Gospel according to:

Priest:

What color are the priest's vestments today?

WHAT I LEARNED

The gospel story was about:

What does God want me to learn?

How should I change because of this homily?

My favorite church song today:

Today I want to pray for:

DRAW A PICTURE OR WRITE SOMETHING
YOU HEARD IN THE GOSPEL

My Sunday Mass Notes

	YES!	NO!
Did you read your Bible this week?	☐	☐
Did you still remember last week's sermon?	☐	☐
Can you say a verse you have learned recently?	☐	☐

Gospel according to: Today's date:

CATCH THE WORD: Check the box each time you hear the word.

☐ God   ☐ Israel   ☐ House
☐ Love   ☐ People   ☐ Day
☐ Jesus   ☐ King   ☐ People
☐ Man   ☐ Son   ☐ Disciples

TODAY'S GOSPEL IS ABOUT..

APPLICATION

I should..

I should not..

DRAW A PICTURE OF SOMETHING YOU HEARD IN THE GOSPEL

My Mass Journal

Today's Date:

Liturgical Calendar:

Responsorial Psalm:

Today I heard the Gospel according to:

How do you attend/watch the mass?

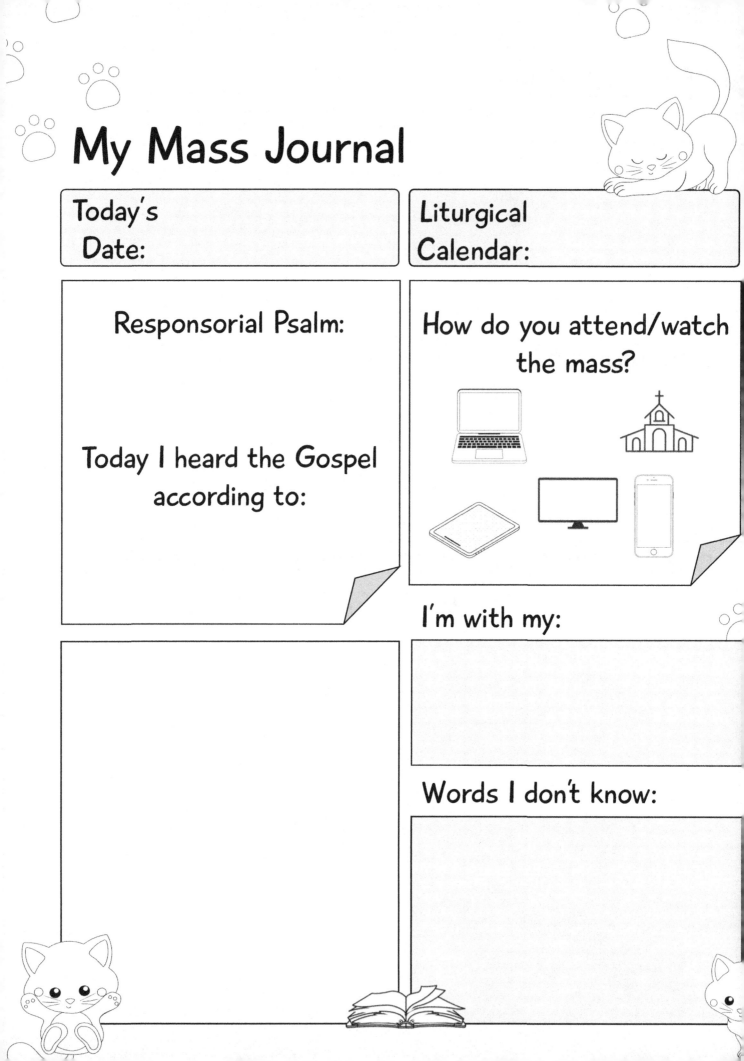

I'm with my:

Words I don't know:

THE PRIEST'S MESSAGE:

3 BIG THINGS I LEARNED TODAY:

DRAW A PICTURE OR WRITE SOMETHING YOU HEARD FROM THE GOSPEL

MASS JOURNAL SHEET

Date: _____

Priest: _____

1st Reading: _____

2nd Reading: _____

WHERE IS THE GOSPEL READING FROM?

_____

3 NAMES OR CHARACTERS I HEARD:

1.

2.

3.

WHAT ARE YOU LEARNING ABOUT GOD FROM THE HOMILY?

I can apply this in my life by..

MY FAVORITE WORSHIP SONG TODAY:

TODAY WE PRAY FOR:

SOMETHING I LEARNED ABOUT MYSELF

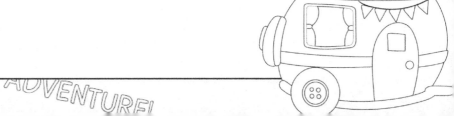

My Sunday Notes

Today's Date:

Gospel according to:

Priest:

What color are the priest's vestments today?

WHAT I LEARNED

The gospel story was about:

What does God want me to learn?

How should I change because of this homily?

BEST NURSE EVER!

My favorite church song today:

Today I want to pray for:

DRAW A PICTURE OR WRITE SOMETHING
YOU HEAR IN THE GOSPEL

HERE
TO HELP!

My Sunday Mass Notes

	YES!	NO!
Did you read your Bible this week?	☐	☐
Did you still remember last week's sermon?	☐	☐
Can you say a verse you have learned recently?	☐	☐

Gospel according to: Today's date:

CATCH THE WORD: Check the box each time you hear the word.

☐ God   ☐ Israel   ☐ House
☐ Love   ☐ People   ☐ Day
☐ Jesus   ☐ King   ☐ People
☐ Man   ☐ Son   ☐ Disciples

TODAY'S GOSPEL IS ABOUT..

APPLICATION

I should..

I should not..

DRAW A PICTURE OF SOMETHING YOU HEARD IN THE GOSPEL

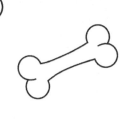
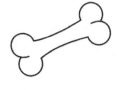

My Mass Journal

Today's Date:

Liturgical Calendar:

Responsorial Psalm:

Today I heard the Gospel according to:

How do you attend/watch the mass?

I'm with my:

Words I don't know:

THE PRIEST'S MESSAGE:

3 BIG THINGS I LEARNED TODAY:

DRAW A PICTURE OR WRITE SOMETHING YOU HEARD FROM THE GOSPEL

MASS JOURNAL SHEET

Date: _____

Priest: _____

1st Reading: _____

2nd Reading: _____

WHERE IS THE GOSPEL READING FROM?

_____

3 NAMES OR CHARACTERS I HEARD:

1.

2.

3.

WHAT ARE YOU LEARNING ABOUT GOD FROM THE HOMILY?

I can apply this in my life by..

MY FAVORITE WORSHIP SONG TODAY:

TODAY WE PRAY FOR:

SOMETHING I LEARNED ABOUT MYSELF

My Sunday Notes

Today's Date:

Gospel according to:

Priest:

What color are the priest's vestments today?

WHAT I LEARNED

The gospel story was about:

What does God want me to learn?

How should I change because of this homily?

I ♡ LONDON

My favorite church song today:

Today I want to pray for:

DRAW A PICTURE OR WRITE SOMETHING
YOU HEARD IN THE GOSPEL

LONDON

My Sunday Mass Notes

	YES!	NO!
Did you read your Bible this week?	☐	☐
Did you still remember last week's sermon?	☐	☐
Can you say a verse you have learned recently?	☐	☐

Gospel according to: Today's date:

CATCH THE WORD: Check the box each time you hear the word.

- ☐ God
- ☐ Love
- ☐ Jesus
- ☐ Man

- ☐ Israel
- ☐ People
- ☐ King
- ☐ Son

- ☐ House
- ☐ Day
- ☐ People
- ☐ Disciples

TODAY'S GOSPEL IS ABOUT..

APPLICATION

I should..

I should not..

DRAW A PICTURE OF SOMETHING YOU HEARD IN THE GOSPEL

My Mass Journal

Today's Date:

Liturgical Calendar:

Responsorial Psalm:

Today I heard the Gospel according to:

How do you attend/watch the mass?

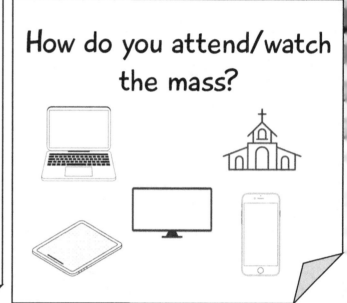

I'm with my:

Words I don't know:

THE PRIEST'S
MESSAGE:

3 BIG THINGS I
LEARNED TODAY:

DRAW A PICTURE OR WRITE SOMETHING YOU
HEARD FROM THE GOSPEL

MASS JOURNAL SHEET

Date:_____   Priest:_____

1st Reading: _____   2nd Reading: _____

WHERE IS THE GOSPEL READING FROM?

_____

3 NAMES OR CHARACTERS I HEARD:

1.
2.
3.

WHAT ARE YOU LEARNING ABOUT GOD FROM THE HOMILY?

I can apply this in my life by..

MY FAVORITE
WORSHIP SONG TODAY:

TODAY WE
PRAY FOR:

SOMETHING I LEARNED ABOUT MYSELF

My Sunday Notes

Today's
Date:

Gospel according to:

Priest:

What color are the priest's vestments today?

WHAT I LEARNED

The gospel story was about:

What does God want me to learn?

How should I change because of this homily?

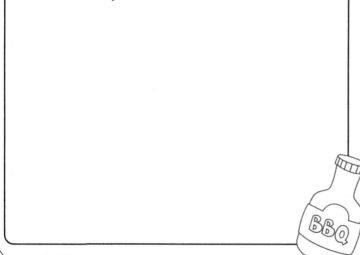

Backyard BBQ

My favorite church song today:

Today I want to pray for:

DRAW A PICTURE OR WRITE SOMETHING
YOU HEARD IN THE GOSPEL

My Sunday Mass Notes

	YES!	NO!
Did you read your Bible this week?	☐	☐
Did you still remember last week's sermon?	☐	☐
Can you say a verse you have learned recently?	☐	☐

Gospel according to: Today's date:

CATCH THE WORD: Check the box each time you hear the word.

❑ God   ❑ Israel   ❑ House
❑ Love   ❑ People   ❑ Day
❑ Jesus   ❑ King   ❑ People
❑ Man   ❑ Son   ❑ Disciples

TODAY'S GOSPEL IS ABOUT..

APPLICATION

I should..

I should not..

DRAW A PICTURE OF SOMETHING YOU HEARD IN THE GOSPEL

My Mass Journal

Today's Date:

Liturgical Calendar:

Responsorial Psalm:

Today I heard the Gospel according to:

How do you attend/watch the mass?

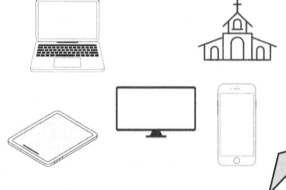

I'm with my:

Words I don't know:

THE PRIEST'S MESSAGE:

3 BIG THINGS I LEARNED TODAY:

DRAW A PICTURE OR WRITE SOMETHING YOU HEARD FROM THE GOSPEL

MASS JOURNAL SHEET

Date:_____   Priest:_____

1st Reading: _____   2nd Reading: _____

WHERE IS THE GOSPEL READING FROM?

_____

3 NAMES OR CHARACTERS I HEARD:

1.

2.

3.

WHAT ARE YOU LEARNING ABOUT GOD FROM THE HOMILY?

I can apply this in my life by..

MY FAVORITE WORSHIP SONG TODAY:

TODAY WE PRAY FOR:

SOMETHING I LEARNED ABOUT MYSELF

My Sunday Notes

Today's
Date:

Gospel according to:

Priest:

What color are the priest's vestments today?

WHAT I LEARNED

The gospel story was about:

What does God want me to learn?

How should I change because of this homily?

My favorite church song today:

Today I want to pray for:

DRAW A PICTURE OR WRITE SOMETHING
YOU HEARD IN THE GOSPEL

My Sunday Mass Notes

	YES!	NO!
Did you read your Bible this week?	☐	☐
Did you still remember last week's sermon?	☐	☐
Can you say a verse you have learned recently?	☐	☐

Gospel according to: Today's date:

CATCH THE WORD: Check the box each time you hear the word.

☐ God   ☐ Israel   ☐ House
☐ Love   ☐ People   ☐ Day
☐ Jesus   ☐ King   ☐ People
☐ Man   ☐ Son   ☐ Disciples

TODAY'S GOSPEL IS ABOUT..

APPLICATION

I should..

I should not..

DRAW A PICTURE OF SOMETHING YOU HEARD IN THE GOSPEL

Made in the USA
Las Vegas, NV
08 March 2024

86894152R00063